UNDERSTANDING HOW TO LIVE FRUITFULLY FOR HIS KINGDOM IN TODAY'S DAY AND AGE

Volume 1

ALTON NORWOOD

Understanding How to Live Fruitfully for His Kingdom in Today's Day and Age
Copyright © 2023 by Alton Norwood. All rights reserved.

No part of this publication may be reproduced, stored in a retrieval system or transmitted in any way by any means, electronic, mechanical, photocopy, recording or otherwise without the prior permission of the author except as provided by USA copyright law.

The opinions expressed by the author are not necessarily those of URLink Print and Media.

1603 Capitol Ave., Suite 310 Cheyenne, Wyoming USA 82001
1-888-980-6523 | admin@urlinkpublishing.com

URLink Print and Media is committed to excellence in the publishing industry.

Book design copyright © 2023 by URLink Print and Media. All rights reserved.

Published in the United States of America
Library of Congress Control Number: 2022900448
ISBN 978-1-68486-074-6 (Paperback)
ISBN 978-1-68486-075-3 (Digital)

20.04.23

UNDERSTANDING HOW TO LIVE FRUITFULLY FOR HIS KINGDOM
IN TODAY'S DAY AND AGE

Contents

Our life is like a big play 7
Introduction 9
Dedication 11
Acknowledgements 13
   Part: 1. Picked out: 15
   Part: 2. Predestinated: 20
   Part: 3. Purpose: 22
Sowing Seeds through the Internet: 25
   Part: 1. The Internet: 26
   Part: 2. Life Itself is a Seed: 33
   Part: 3. Sowing Seeds through Giving: 35
The Apostolic Age 37
   Part: 1. Illumination: 39
   Part: 2. Revelations: 41
   Part: 3. The 3 Lenses 43
   Part: 4. let's look at Rightly Dividing
      the word of truth: 44
   Part: 5. The Apostles: 48
   Part: 6. The Gifts: 54

Preparing to Meet the Millennium Reign 61
   Part: 1. Accountability of the Saints: 63
   Part 2. Rewards: 68
   Part: 3. Judgment of the Nations: 70

Rules in The Kingdom of Heaven 75
   Part: 1. Dispensations: 75
   Part: 2. Kingdom of God: 79
   Part: 3. Kingdom of Heaven: 79

The Curse of Nature 84
   Part: 1. The Creator: 85
   Part: 2. The Creature: 88
   Part: 3. The Curse of Nature: 89

Our life is like a big play

By Reverend Alton Norwood Sr.

Table of contents:

Part: 1. Picked Out:
Part: 2. Predestinated:
Part: 3. Purpose:

Introduction

God gave man the ideal to make plays our whole life is like one big play God is the Producer and Director we are the actors on Gods screen just playing out our role. What man is doing on TV God gave him that ideal for a reason in the natural. but Spiritually it points to our Life. And as God give it to me, I will give it to you. Our Faith Puts us on Center Stage

In Hebrews: Chapter: 10. verse 33. Says Partly, whilst ye were made a gazing stock- means- in the Greek text where we get the word theater – means to observe, watch, study, to bring upon stage to see. This is our new stand on the word of God it puts us on center stage. The stage called The Play of Life.

Now the stage is set the actors is in place the play is being watched just like man watch plays or movies. God is watching us play out his play he knows how it will end he is the producer, director, and writer. the film is rolling every day we live.

Dedication

To my Wife: Alberta Norwood, My Daughter: Marshaun Ford, My Son Alton Norwood Jr, To my Son in Law: Rodney the Captain Ford. And all of my Grand Children Breana Ford, Brittani Ford, Briley Ford, Alton Norwood 3rd Trey, Kahmauri Norwood, and Asher Norwood.

Acknowledgements

To Dr. George W. Dollar: May 12, 1917 – January 17, 2006 The Lord has called him home my Instructor and Bible Teacher. The Lord Thru him open my eyes through the Scripture.

In 1ˢᵗ Corinthians Chapter: 2. Verse. 14. Says But the natural man receiveth not the things of the Spirit of God: for they are foolishness unto him: neither can he know them because they are spiritually discerned – means the unsaved cannot see he is like a blind man walking around. Until the Light shine into his heart and he accept Jesus Christ as his Savior.

Part: 1. Picked out:

You been chosen means- God has picked you out to carry out his script like man a producer picks their actors for special part's. God choose individuals for a special office.

In 1st Corinthians: Chapter. 1. Verse. 27. But God hath chosen the foolish things- means a person who we think that do not have the ability or not capable to do something but when God saves you, he gifts you with a spiritual gift.

Example where you were not a speaker you are now. This is not a natural gift but a spiritual gift.

Verse 27. continues of this world to confound the wise; - means the person that could speak or had boldness in the natural or can do all manner of things but now they can see you can speak well for God. That is amazing to them now to see what you have become in God.

Verse continues 27. And God hath chosen- means picked you out the weak- means the least notice or what you consider ignorant things- means people of the world the verse continues saying, to confound the things which are mighty- means the geniuses.

In Ephesians: Chapter: 1. Verse 4. Says According as he hath chosen- means picked or selected us in him before the foundation of the world, these are the elect of God- the chosen ones- means saved ones the verse continues that we should be holy and without blame before him in love.

Now let's look at Election- means God selects you to salvation takes place in Christ as part of his plan. God allow us to use our freedom to rebel against him God is gracious to save those who find him it is not unjust of him not to save everyone since no one deserves to be saved.

In Romans: Chapter. 1. Verse 18. For the wrath of God is revealed from heaven against all ungodliness and unrighteousness of men, who hold the truth in unrighteousness; apart from Gods sovereign choice of sinners to become his children, none would be saved but remain forever under his wrath.

In Romans: Chapter. 9.verse 15. For he saith to Moses, I will have mercy on whom I will have mercy, and I will have compassion on whom I will have compassion.

And the same today God have mercy on whom he will and he have compassion on whom he will No matter how bad your child is if God choose to have mercy on them it will be his choice.

Some children are better than yours and they don't get the chance yours get it's the mercy of God on who he will. mercy- is something that we don't deserve we all deserve death but God had mercy on us.

Its Gods Election: - is the Sovereign Will of God who cannot change means- God picks and choose whom he wants whether we like it or not because God see the beginning and the ending of our lives.

We may see a child as a good child but God see where he will turn to be a bad child and we may see a child as bad child but God see where he will turn to be a good child.

That's why God is sovereign and we are not. this is Gods play of Life he knows the Beginning and the Ending we do not and remember it began the moment we were born, or in the womb.

In Romans: Chapter. 8. Verse. 29. For whom he did foreknow-means- it was already planned he knew it before it happen verse continues; he also did predestinate- means- he preplanned it he planned it before means- its rigged or a setup we just don't know it but God does.

In 2nd Thessalonians: Chapter. 2. Verse. 13. But we are bound to give thanks always to God for you, brethren beloved of the Lord, because God hath from the beginning chosen you- means this is the sovereign will of God to salvation through sanctification of the Spirit and belief of the truth: Salvation of the elect is certain. The Elect choose God because he calls them through the gospel and because he first chose and called them to himself.

In Romans: Chapter. 8. Verse. 28. And we know that all things work together for the good-means God work all things together for the good that means death, troubles, situations whatever it may be to them that love God, to them who are the called-means, chosen, handpicked, verse continues according to his purpose.

The elect believes but do not believe against their will they have a God given desire and ability to trust in Christ for salvation.

In Romans: Chapter. 8. Verse. 33. Who shall lay anything to the charge of Gods elect? It is God that justifieth.

Man, human will- is free to choose for or against God those who are slaves to sin and its power

In Romans: Chapter: 6. Verse. 6. Knowing this, that our old man is crucified with him, that the body of sin might be destroyed, that henceforth we should not serve sin.

Neither understand nor seek after God. In Romans: Chapter: 3. Verse. 11. There is none that understandeth, there is none that seeketh after God.

Outside of Christ people are spiritually dead who neither desire to submit to the Lord nor are able to. In Romans: Chapter 1. Verse. 18 Apart from Gods Sovereign choice of sinners to become his children, none would be saved but would remain forever under his wrath In.

Genesis: Chapter: 1. Verse. 26. And God said, let us- means the father, son and the holy Ghost make man in our image, after our likeness: before God created man and the Earth, he had a blueprint already just like man does before they build a building, or prepare a Play or Movie, He has to put everything in place and get the people he needs to act in the film that what God did before he made man, he had thought it out already.

Man was handpicked before he made the earth. Satan was picked to deceive God but he didn't know it but God did because God is omnipotent – means he knows all things but Satan do not there is nothing that God don't know means you are picked to play your part in God's Play of Life.

Part: 2. Predestinated:

Means- it's Preplanned- planned before. anything that's planned out is Rigged. you already know how it will end up its fixed. just like a play you just have to play out your script it's already written God wrote it. there is no coincidence God has preplanned or predestinated- means- prearranged everything. means- it's Rigged he already knows the end of the Play of Life we just have to act it out.

In Ephesians: Chapter: 1. Verse 5. Says Having predestinated us unto the adoption of children by Jesus Christ to himself, according to the good pleasures of his will,

In Acts: Chapter: 2. Verse. 23 here's predestination and freewill in one verse. God plan Jesus Death and man carried it out.

Verse. 23. Him, being delivered by the determine counsel and foreknowledge- means he knew before its rigged. of God, verse continues ye have taken, and by wicked hands have crucified and slain: this is part of Gods Play of Life it had to end in death or you live. But not everybody will die. Just like in man's play some die in the play but some live to.

Yes, In Hebrews: Chapter: 9. Verse. 27. Says And as it is appointed unto men once to die, but after this the judgement: it doesn't mean everybody will die you just haven't studied enough. you have to read a little further. some of us will not die a natural death. some will be alive when Jesus comes back for the saints.

In 1st Thessalonians: Chapter: 4. verse 15. For this we say unto you by the word of the Lord, that we which are alive and remain unto the coming of the Lord shall not prevent them which are asleep.

Verse. 16. For the Lord himself shall descend from heaven with a shout, with the voice of the archangel, and with the trump of God: and the dead in Christ shall rise first:

verse. 17. Then we which are alive and remain shall be caught up together with them in the clouds, to meet the Lord in the air: and so, shall we ever be with the Lord.

Yes, some will die and some will live in The Play of Life. we just don't know who and when but God does because he wrote, produced, and directed the script in The Play of Life. This is our life it just has to be played out and it will in its time. Also, some will be saved and some will be lost.

Part: 3. Purpose:

In this Play of Life God has a purpose for everybody that's born on this earth you are no accident because God chose you. He selected you for a special task or a special part in his play just like man pick actors for certain parts in a play. Romans: 8. Verse 28. Says to them who are the called according to- his purpose means we all have a purpose in life we just have to find it. I know mine now.

In Psalms: 139. Verse. 15. Says My substance was hid from thee, when I was made in secret, and curiously wrought in the lowest parts of the earth.

Verse. 16. Thine eyes did see my substance yet being unperfect; and in thy book all my members were written, which in continuance were fashioned, when as yet there was none of them. Gods eyes was on us in the earliest stage of being form.

No human is a surprise to God. You are part of his plan. every step of man and women is order by the Lord.

In Psalms: 37. Verse. 23. Says The steps of a good man are ordered by the Lord: and he delighted in his way.

So, there is no coincidence. where you go or reside it part of The Play of Life it meant to be its part of Gods script. We all have a purpose in The Play of Life even the wicked-unsaved they have to play out their wickedness and the Righteous their Righteousness.

Now I know my purpose in Gods script. After all these years that's why I am writing this book so God can show you your part in The Play of Life. we been playing our role since we were born in this life; we just didn't know it then it took time but God let me know everybody should know their part in The Play of Life.

In man's play you do so what about Gods Play you should too, that's why we have to find our purpose of being on earth. we all have a script in the Play of Life. And after you read my book, I pray that God open your eyes so you can see your part in the Play of Life. whether it's Righteous or unrighteous we all have a purpose in the script. we are already carrying it out even if we don't know it. you are in the Play of Life.

I Pray that God give you Illuminations- means to open your eyes so you can see what God is saying to you in this Book the Play of Life. May God Bless your Heart and soul.

Sowing Seeds through the Internet:

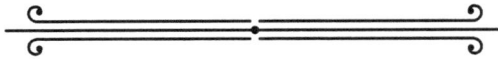

Table of Contents:

Part: 1. The Internet:
Part: 2. Life Itself is a Seed:
Part: 3. Sowing Seeds through Giving:

Introduction: New Technology has changed our world so much if we do not adapt to the changes we will be left behind. we must adapt to change in this changing world.

<u>This includes our 3 Types of Lives:</u>

1. Work life: - at work
2. Home life: - at home
3. Church life: - at Church and we have to separate them.

We have to make changes and know where to make changes in this modern world. we been at it for hundreds of years every time a new invention comes out, or an improvement to one, hundreds, perhaps thousands of people lose their jobs.

It seems the more we get, the more we want, From Benjamin Franklin discovering electricity to Thomas Edison and the light bulb to Henry Ford and the automobile to the Wright Brother and flight to the Cotton Gun in the south to radio and television to Alexander Graham Bell and the telephone to Bill Gates and the Computer We are advancing ourselves right out of jobs.

Machines and Technology are taking their toll on the jobless. and here we are today the Internet. which has Face book, Twitter, Instagram, LinkedIn, etc. you have a lot of names on the Internet. today you can pick what you like. to me all of them is a tool to reach people all over the world within in seconds. And a way to sow seeds into your life. Yet they all have the devil's playground on them stay away from it.

Part: 1. The Internet:

Some use it for the devil's playground such as gossips, porn, pictures, etc. but I use it as a tool to communicate Spiritually and Naturally just like sowing seeds. every tweet I tweet to me is like a seed sown in the earth. And every word falls in your garden and I believe it will come up in its season. God's timing could be a day, month, or years but it right on time. Just Like a farmer.

In Mark: Chapter- 4 verse 26. Says And he said, so is the kingdom of God, as if a man should cast seed into the ground:

Verse 27. And should sleep, and rise night and day, and the seed should spring and grow up, he knoweth not how.

Verse-28. For the earth bringeth forth fruit of herself; first the blade, then the ear, after that the full corn in the ear.

Verse 29. But when the fruit is brought forth, immediately he putteth in the sickle, because the harvest is come.

This is your break through now we need to have patience of a farmer he plants his seeds they say it take a year before his harvest comes up.

Now we can all be farmers we don't have to envy anybody that's being blessed because there is plenty of room for you to plant- means your ideas, thoughts, goals and visions all off these are seeds you just have to sow- plant like the farmer does.

Put your seeds out there your ideas and thoughts. there is a lot of farmers planting their crop everyday- like there is a lot of people that have visions and goals and there is some not planting but if you are not planting blame yourself you will not receive much you have to make it happen it's not coming to you go get it.

I been sowing- means doing something for years you may not see it yet just like a seed you plant you don't see what's going on under the ground yet but wait and see until it come up. That's your season that's your harvest it takes time patience is the key.

The more seeds -means all of those tweets I tweeted the more will come up we call this a breakthrough they have to come up because I sowed them Those tweets, I had already sowed them but the time hadn't come up yet it may take a while the seed was in the ground everything was getting prepared before it come up.

That's what God does for us, we are in the waiting stage he is getting everything ready putting every person in place for you to meet and then he will give you your harvest.

When God made man, he had made everything before he made man and for man then he put everything in place for man before he put man in the garden.

Why. Because man couldn't survive if he had made man first, he put everything around man first then he made man.

Man needed sustainability like we do so God put things in place for you so you can sustain your vision and dream and now You're ready for your harvest- means your blessing. Your season is ready then.

If you sow a little you should expect a little but if you don't so anything don't expect anything. some people will not receive a harvest so don't be envious when you see others people seeds- means blessing coming up don't be envious just start sowing- means doing something and you will receive your harvest

It's your choice God give us all a choice we can serve him or not we can work or not. If you don't sow you will not reap. you cannot expect a harvest if you didn't sow anything Every person knows what he has sown.

So, I expect a big harvest. I been tweeting hundreds, thousands of tweets-these are all seeds and now it's time for them to come up. this is the harvest for sowing it's coming up now.

Donations is coming in, Fundraising, Grants now. This is what the Holy Spirit has given to me about Sowing Seeds through the Internet. this is a Spiritual meaning of the Internet in the Natural world and as he gives it to me, I will give it to you.

We say we are waiting on God but no God is waiting on us. if we don't move God will not either. In James: Chapter 4. Verse 8. Says draw nigh to God he will draw nigh to you. Means -The saying if you make one step, he will make two.

In Matthews: Chapter 13. Jesus spake in parables because of the multitudes were their he knew they would not understand.

In Verse 3. And he spake many things unto them in parables, -means a truth concealed but now being revealed. The verse continues saying, behold a sower went forth to sow;

Verse 4. And when he sowed, some seeds fell by the way side, -means the crowd verse continues and the fowls came and devoured them up: - means the wicked one catcheth that which was sown in heart and steal it. don't let the devil steal your thought or ideal.

Verse 5. Some fell upon stony places, where they had not much earth: and for with they sprung up, because they had no deepness of the earth:

Verse 6. And when the sun was up, they were scorched; and because they had no root, they withered away. means this is a person who hear the word of God with joy but has not root in himself and when tribulations come because of the word he is offended. He doesn't last because he has no root in him.

Verse 7. And some fell among thorns; and the thorns sprung up and choked them: - means this is the cares of this world, riches choke the word and he became unfruitful.

Let me tell you what the holy spirit gave to me. This means you are sowing in the wrong area of life -thorns and thistles- means in the natural you are asking the wrong people for funding or donations. This is a waste of time because the ground is not good ground. so, sow - tweet other Billionaires that will donate to your cause.

Verse 8. But other fell into good ground, and brought forth fruit, some an hundredfold, some sixty-fold, some thirty-fold. -this is he who heareth the word and understand it.

this was the disciples they understood Jesus parables they were the good soil. But the crowds could not understand them. - So, this is the Spiritual understanding of Jesus parable in Matthew: Chapter 13.

But now I want to share with you the natural meaning that came to me by the Holy Spirit. we know today the

Preacher is the sower he is Preaching the word and it's falling on all types of Soils-means people.

Some receive it and some don't. I thought about the Internet I usually don't get on it because it so much mess on it but I thought about it and I said I can live in this world all around trouble but I don't have to get involved in it.

So, I said I can use the Internet to Sow Seeds Spiritually to help someone. and don't' have to get involved in the other stuff- the devil's playground. that's what I' am doing every tweet I expect something will come back.

I like the Pastors Discussion on LinkedIn and Twitter. it has helped a lot of people all over the world with their problems and questions. This is a tool to reach people all over the world quickly. This is why I use it to do the Lords work and be blessed. The problem is just like in Matthew: Chapter 13. We are sowing in the wrong places.

Example if you want money or Donations you don't go to the poor -or tweet the poor you tweet the rich- I mean the Billionaires that have money that is the good soil then you can expect your seed to come up.

You have to sow or tweet the right people-is soil to get results. Even Millionaires know that they have their foundations but they go to the Billionaires for support.

That's why it hard for me and you and other organization to get funds. Because the Millionaires are getting them. So, I don't go to the Millionaires I go straight to the Billionaires the Top 10. I ask them that is the good soil. That's the right place to look.

In Proverbs Chapter 13. Verse 22. A good man leaveth an inheritance to his children's children: and the wealth of the sinner is laid up for the just. I believe that God will touch the hearts of the rich. the Bill Gates, Amancio Ortega, Warren Buffets, Carlos Slim Helu, etc. if you are a just man wealth is laid up for you. but you have to ask- means sow a seed if you don't you want receive it.

Part: 2. Life Itself is a Seed:

Everything you do in life is like sowing a seed. Whether it's good or bad it comes back to you. we call it karma- means what goes around comes around. but the Bible calls it Reaping and Sowing.

In Galatians: Chapter: 6. verse 7. Be not deceived; God is not mocked: for whatsoever a man -or women soweth, that shall he also reap. Means what you sow whether it's good or bad comes back to you. that's why you should sow good every day no matter how someone treat you treat them good. You will reap good back in life.

In Proverbs: Chapter: 25. Verse 21. If thine enemy be hungry, give him bread to eat; and if he be thirsty, give him water to drink: - Means treat your enemy right even if he treats you wrong.

Verse. 22. For thou shalt heap coals of fire upon his head, and the Lord shall reward thee. - means Just treat him right it will bother him don't' worry about its God will take care of it. If you sow bad you will reap bad.

Let go back to Galatians: Chapter: 6. Verse. 8. For he that soweth to his flesh shall of the flesh reap corruption; - means you will reap it while you are here in the flesh before you die. the verse continues but he that soweth to the Spirit shall of the Spirit reap life everlasting. – means in the future with God.

So, our life is like planting seeds in the ground every day. And it will come up in your life now. Also, we sow seeds in our giving.

Part: 3. Sowing Seeds through Giving:

In 2nd Corinthians: Chapter 9. Verse 6. Says But this I say, He which soweth sparingly- means a little. shall reap also sparingly; - a little. Verse continues and he which soweth bountifully- means a lot. Verse continues shall reap also bountifully- means a lot. if I give a little expect a little back. If I give a lot. expect a lot back.

The Bible says in Matthews: Chapter 7. Verse 7. Ask, and it shall be given you; - means you don't just ask one time it means keep on asking. This is a seed you are sowing. Verse continues Seek, - means keep on seeking, and ye shall find; verse continue Knock- means keep on knocking, verse continue and it shall be opened unto you: - it's like planting seeds keep on planting seeds you will see seeds. -results this has to be the will of God. This is the condition.

In James: chapter 4. Verse 3. Ye ask, and receive not, - means but there is a condition. Verse continues Because ye ask amiss, that ye may consume it upon your lust. -means you ask and wanted it to be pleased. Did you want it because God wanted you to have it or you just wanted it?

I believe if I need a Million Dollars God will let me get it. But not because I want it but I need it to do his work.

So, I' am sowing seeds all over the internet and I expect a big harvest. May God touch your hearts to sow to our ministry.

The Apostolic Age

By Reverend Alton Norwood, Sr.

We pray that God open up your eyes of understanding.

Table of Contents:

Part: 1. Illuminations:
Part: 2. Revelations:
Part: 3. The 3 Lenses:
Part: 4. Rightly Dividing the Word of Truth:
Part: 5. The Apostles:
Part: 6. The Gifts of the Spirit:

Introduction: The Apostolic Age: this is the 1st period of Church History it begins at the Church in the time of Jesus 30 Ad. And Ends with the Apostle John on the Isle of Patmos in 95 Ad.

Nero Killed Paul & Peter died in 64 Ad. Martyr in Rome they were accused of setting a fire the emperor in Rome in the time of Nero. Nero lived until 68 Ad.

The Book of Acts: is the history of the church it's the only book that's church history a book of what Jesus done & taught.

Now let's look at a good Church. you have to have 3 things.

1. Message- The Word of God
2. Messenger- Pastor
3. Method. - A Structure

Churches today need these 3 things they need good structure to be productive in today's day and age you need more than worship you need youth minister's recreation programs etc. because times has change churches has to adapt in these times we live in now. Let's look at the book of Acts: is title the originals call it the Acts of the Holy Apostles.

In Acts: Chapter 1. verse 3. the word alive -means these are infallible proofs means- without error the Apostles was eyewitnesses they witness the life and times of Jesus. They literally seen him me and you have not that's why they are called Apostles -means- they seen the Lord there is no Apostles today. Luke wrote the book of Acts.

Let talk a little about Bible College. Now Some people are against school let's look at the word {theology}

-means a study of God Theo-means God and ology-means study.

So, School sharpens you and these are your tool's you may not use them much while you are going to school but go and get them you will use them later after you finish school that's what I'm doing now that's why I can write my book's now I got my tool's when I went to school. Example What good is a mechanic without tool.

In Acts: chapter 19. Verse 9&10 they had schools during the time of the early church Paul separated the disciples, disputing daily in the School of one Tyrannus. Ver10. And this continued by the space of two years; so that all they which dwelt in Asia heard the word of the Lord Jesus, both Jew and Greeks. So, in this Book, these are some of my nuggets I have to offer to you. I pray that God Illuminate your hearts and minds.

Part: 1. Illumination:

This word means- to shed light. example if you are in a room and the lights is off there are many pictures in the building but you cannot see them because the lights are off. until you turn on the lights you cannot see the pictures.

Example when you get into your automobile at night you turn on your Illuminators- means lights that's the way the Bible is. we pray that you have an open heart and mind and let the spirit of God Illuminate your understanding.

The Bible says in 1st Corinthians: Chapter: 2. verse 14. the natural man receiveth not the things of God. For they are foolish to him. this is why you must have the Holy Spirit in you. the Holy Spirit knows the Holy Spirit. if it's in you it will turn on the lights of understanding this is Illuminations- which means it already been there the lights just had to be turned on so you can see. The unsaved cannot see this until he accepts Jesus as Lord & Savior then the light is turned on.

You can read 1st Corinthians: chapter: 2. verse 10-14 to shed more light on your understanding.

Now let's look at revelations there is no more Revelations- which mean to reveal or unveil something that was never there. But there is Illuminations -means it is already there. the spirit has to turn the lights on so you can understand the Scriptures.

Part: 2. Revelations:

Means to reveal or unveiling. the Apostolic Age begin at the time of Jesus 30 ad. End with the Apostle John 95 ad. the gifts went out.

Then Paul said in 1st Corinthians: Chapter: 13. verse 9. for we know in part and we prophesy in part Paul was saying that he only had partial knowledge of the scriptures in his day they only had the Old Testament then.

The New Testament was in the making they was making it then when he said this. they didn't have the complete Bible when he said this, they had partial knowledge of the cannon that's why he said in verse 9. Paul said Prophecies, they shall fail, tongues shall cease knowledge, shall vanish away and it has today.

Verse 10. Says But when that is perfect is come that which in part is done away with. Which mean you will have the complete cannon.

Today we have the complete Bible. the Old Testament was written in Hebrew and the New Testament was written in Greek. So, you have to go back to the original language to get the meaning of the word.

Example just like a TV black & white or colored the Greek & Hebrew is the true color to the Scriptures it points out anything that's false just like you detect counterfeit money.

Let's talk about the gifts a little now 6 of those gifts was temporal- means to get them started just like a foundation you build on a house and 13 was permanent total of 19.

During Paul's day the Corinthian church was immature these gifts was given to them to help them reach maturity. so today you don't need all of these gifts because we have the complete Revelation which is the Bible the 66 books you read that's your revelation.

The Apostles in 2nd Peter: Chapter: 1. verse 21. For Prophecy came not in old time by the will of man. But Holy men of God spake as they were moved by the Holy Ghost.

Prophecy came direct from God to the Apostles they were holy men spake - God breathe God literally took control of their mouth and told them what to write. this is what we got today and what we read in the New Testament this is the Revelation God left for man to read. there will be no more revelations we have it in the 66 books of the Bible.

In Hebrews: Chapter: 1. verse 1. Says God who at sundry- means varies times and divers- means different manners spake in time past unto the fathers- means Moses them verse continues by the Prophets under law- means that was the Dispensation of Law.

Verse 2. hath in these last days- means under Grace today that's a different Dispensation. we are under it now which means he speaks differently now he speaks through his Son.

Part: 3. The 3 Lenses

The lenses are Gods Revelation to man, people say the Bible is God's love letter to man & women. He loved us, so he left us a roadmap or a GPS to show us how to get to him this is your Bible the 66 Books.

So, the 1st Lens- is the Lens of Scripture: -your Bible 66 books

2nd The Lens of History: -we have to go back into the Bible day who, what, when it was said lets us know the history.

3rd. The Lens of Cultural: - how they lived what it meant in their day you see the whole bible is already interpreted we just have to go back into that day and learn what it was referring to in that day.

Example the Bible says in Matthew: Chapter; 19. verse 24. it easier for a camel to go through the eye of a needle than for a rich man to go to heaven.

Culture tells you that referred to a Needles Eye- was a gate where a camel had to kneel down in order to go under the gate because the hump on his back. that hump today is the rich man riches.

It hard for him to humble himself but some will. not all rich people will be lost. So, this is the true interpretation of that scripture this is how we should preach it.

God doesn't have to come down and reveal to us like he did to the Apostles he left it here. in 95 Ad. Was the last Revelation to man & women through the Apostle John in the Book of Revelation. John said I am Alpha and Omega the Beginning and the Ending the First & the Last.

Part :4. let's look at Rightly Dividing the word of truth:

In 2nd Timothy: Chapter: 2. verse 15. Says Study to show thyself approved unto God, a workman that needed not to be ashamed, rightly dividing the Word of truth —

Example a steak you cannot eat a steak whole it has to be cut up so you can digest it. that's the way the Bible is people try to take the whole Bible and apply it to them but no when you read a passage find out who it talking to. Some things are not talking to us today.

let's look at 3 Things the Bible talks to:

1. The Jews- is the Jew
2. Gentile- is believers Today
3. Church- is all believers neither Jew or Gentile but all believers in Jesus Christ.

You can apply any passage to you today. example will God open the Red Sea today like he did in Moses day. No but we can say God will make a way when we come to our Red Seas in our life.

Now there are 3. thing we must do when reading the Scriptures.

1. Exegeses - means to draw out the Scriptures like you take a rag and ring it out you get all the water you can get out of it. that's the way you do the Scriptures. you tear that text apart get the meaning of every word don't leave nothing out of the text.

2. Eisegeses-means they add to the Scriptures. how they think in their mind what they think the Scriptures mean.

   God is not going to come down and speak to you out of the air. If you are waiting on him to give you a Revelation it's not coming why because he has already left it to you through the 3 Lenses.

   I use to think that to but thank God he let me meet good Teacher in Bible class. So, there is only 1 Revelation and that's your Bible the 66 Books. and God don't need to reveal that again because he already sent it.

   So, don't believe that what people say that there is a New Revelation not so there is only 1 Revelation and that is your Bible the 66 books. And he is not going to Reveal it again he done it through the Apostles and it ended with John in Revelation that's your last Revelation.

3. Apogeses- means they missed the mark. Just like shooting at a target and don't hit anything. Some people miss the whole picture and meaning of the word.

Now There is 3. rules in teaching:

1. Repeat

2. Repeat
3. Repeat.

You get it there is no more Revelations it's here in your Bible the 66 books. The Bible says in Matthew: chapter: 5. verse 6. he that hunger and thirst after righteousness shall be filled. You may be like me I was hungry to know what the word means and he answered my prayer through my Bible Instructors.

Remember this reading makes a full man or women and then you can empty out. So, don't say like a lot of people say all you have to do is open your mouth and God will fill it. Not so he will fill it with hot air. you have to study and then you can empty out just like I'am doing now. if you are full it comes out. if not, nothing comes out. So, you have to know how to approach the Bible when you pick it up.

God left his Revelation to us today through the 3 Lenses. he is not coming down out of the sky to you it's already here. You just got to dig for it through the 3 lenses you cannot be lazy. The Bible is like a Gold Mine you have to dig deep to find the treasure. You have to leave the surface and dig deep. that's the way the Bible Is.

Part :5. The Apostles:

This is the shortest period in church history of all periods. God is the penman he spoke to the Apostles and they wrote the Revelation the New Testament for us from 30 Ad. To 95 Ad. 65 years he moved Miraculously.

This takes me to Matthews: Chapter: 10. This was the ordination service to the twelve Apostles not to us. They were ordained to do these things in Matthew: 10. These are the original 12 Apostles.

The Apostle Paul came later to the Gentiles in Acts chapter: 9. verse 1-5 God stopped Saul who was later Paul from persecuting the disciples and called him the light shined upon him. that light has to shine upon you today so you can see the things of God.

These men mission was to the Jews only. in Matthew: Chapter: 10. verse 1. And when he had called unto him his twelve disciples-which is the twelve Apostles he gave them power against unclean spirits, to cast them out, and to heal all manner of sickness and all manner of disease. All twelve Apostles had this power in that day.

But here is the problem today we apply this to us today that wrong Application. You cannot take the whole

Bible and put it on you. all the Bible is not talking to you just like you cannot take a steak and eat it whole it has to be cut up so is the Bible.

1st you need to know who it talking to.

2nd what it talking about.

3rd. when it was said.

So, we need to cut it strait. let's Exegete the Scripture not Apogee- means you miss the mark or target let's cut it strait. he never told no Preacher today to do these things in Matthew: chapter: 10. this was to the original twelve. and their names is in verse 2-4 this was their mission. Not ours.

In verse 5. These twelve Jesus sent forth, and commanded them, saying, go not into the way of the gentiles, - your mission is not to the gentiles and into any city of the Samaritans enter ye not:

Verse 6. But go rather to the lost sheep of the house of Israel. -this is the Jews their mission was limited to only the Jews of their day.

Verse 7. And as ye go, Preach, saying, The Kingdom of Heaven is at hand the Kingdom of Heaven-is the Millennium Kingdom and Jesus was ready to set up his Millennium Kingdom if the Jews had repented but they rejected him so he didn't set it up.

So, he turned to the Gentiles. Paul comes along later in the New Testament and the Gentiles is grafted in. Romans: chapter: 11. verse 19. we were grafted in. the Jews rejecting God made away for the Gentiles.

In Romans: chapter: 11. verse 24. who were a wild olive tree- this is the Gentiles? broken off-these were the Jews. that I may be graffed in-these are the Gentiles. Jesus made a way for the Gentiles to be saved.

Let's look at the word thousand years. The Latin word for Thousand Years Millennium in Revelation: Chapter: 20. verse 2 - 7 Mille" - means Thousand and "Annum" - means years put them together Mille-Annum -means Millennium but now he will set it up in the future because the Jews rejected him.

Let's go back to Matthew: 10. Verse 8. Says Heal the sick, yes God heals today. But these twelve had the power to heal in that day but not us today.

In James: Chapter 5. Verse 14. Is any sick among you. Let him call for the elders of the church and let them pray over him anointing him with oil in the name of the Lord.

Verse 15. And the prayer of faith shall save the sick, and the Lord shall raise him up, so today we pray the prayer of faith and the Lord heals them if it's his will. But in their day if any one of the Apostles touched you, they had the power to heal you this is how you knew who an Apostle was. they did signs and wonders. Cleanse the lepers, raise the dead- they had power to raise the dead.

Paul did it Acts: Chapter 2. verse 43. many signs and wonders were done by the Apostle.

In Acts: Chapter 3. verse 7. Peter took the lame man by the hand and lift him up and immediately his feet and ancle received strength they had the power to heal Jesus gave it to them as Peter ministry was coming to a close Paul was coming on the seen this is our man today, he was to the Gentiles.

<u>Let look at the 3 lines of Abraham</u>:

1. Flesh line- the Jews
2. Folly line- when he went into Hagar this is where the Arabs come from
3. Faith line-this is us today we are Abraham's seed by faith

In Matthews: 10. when he called them. this is where Preachers today get this from saying they should do the same thing but not so this was talking to the 12 Apostles only you get it. we will tell you about our mission later in Matthew: chapter 28. okay. nobody today is doing that in Matthew: 10. today.

In Acts: Chapter 5. verse 15. they brought the sick in the streets in beds and as Peter passed by his shadow overshadow them, they were healed. If you were an Apostle you could do that. Paul in Acts: Chapter 19. verse 11& 12 Paul was given a Healing Ministry but today you don't have that.

In Verse 11. And God wrought special miracles by the hands of Paul:

Verse 12. So that from his body were brought unto the sick handkerchiefs or aprons, and the diseases departed from them, and the evil spirits went out of them. Preachers try to duplicate this but it not happening today.

Paul in Acts: Chapter 20. verse 9. there sat a widow a certain young man named Eutychus, being fallen into a deep sleep: and as Paul was long Preaching, he sunk down with sleep, and fell down from the third loft: taken up dead.

Verse 10. And Paul went down, and fell on him, embracing him said, trouble not yourself; for his life is in him.

Verse 12. said and they brought the young man alive. Paul, he raised the dead he had the power to do that all Apostle had that power in that day.

Jesus gave it to them in Matthew 10. if you read the book of Acts the Apostles did many more signs and wonders.

In Matthew: Chapter 10. they got this power but not today so do not apply this to you today.

Today there are no more Apostles they ended in Revelation the Apostle John was the last one. So, you see this was never talking to us today.

Our mission came in Matthew: Chapter 28. verse 19&20.

after Jesus had died and rose again, he came and spake to the disciples this is our mission today. This is the great commission.

Verse 19. Go ye therefore, and teach all nations, - means this is a mission to all the world not like Matthew 10. the Apostles mission was limited to the Jews only ours is extended to all the world that's the difference.

Also, he didn't tell us here to heal the sick, raised the dead etc. like he told them in Matthew 10.

This is what he ordained us to do today. The verse continues Baptizing them in the name of the Father, and of the Son, and of the Holy Ghost:

Verse 20. Teaching them to observe all things whatsoever I have commanded you: and, lo, I am with you always, even unto the end of the world. Amen. Remember the only ordinance we are required to do is Baptism and the Lord Supper in the New Testament.

Part: 6. The Gifts:

These are the Chapters all of the Gifts are in 13 were permanent and 6 were temporal it was 19 total gifts. Let's lists the Gifts.

In 1st Corinthians: Chapter 12. verse 8. these are Divine:

For to one is given by the Spirit the word of wisdom; -this is the wisdom of God.

To another the word of Knowledge- the Knowledge of God we have these 2 today.

Verse 9. to another faith-you have Gift of Faith

to another the gift of healing you do not have today.

The Apostles had this Gifts only. Jesus gave it to them in Matthew 10. if they touched you were healed. today we pray the prayer of faith and if its Gods will he heal you. the Apostles had this power but we don't have it today.

Verse 10. To another the working of miracles; -not today they are gone to.

prophecy; -you don't have today.

to another discerning of spirits; -this is Discernment of the word. You have this today.

To another diver's kind of tongues; -different languages you don't have today.

To another the interpretation of tongues; not today.

But what we do have today is people that know languages of the earth who can translate what language you talk in. When you speak in foreign countries, they translate what you say that's interpretation and tongues is a language of the earth. you speak to people that know languages of the earth can interpret it. that's what tongues & interpretation is today.

In Ephesians: Chapter 4. verse 11. Paul says These are the agents of the Lord 5 gifts of the Lord so we can walk worthy.

Apostles; -he gave some apostles -New Testament one's not today. all Apostles seen the Lord even Paul who was not of the original 12 in Matthew: Chapter 10 he came on later but he seen the Lord if you were an Apostle means you have seen the Lord not today there is no more.

And some Prophets, New Testament prophet's they ended with the New Testament. No more today.

They say they are but the word of God is our Prophet

today we have the Revelation in the 66 books today the Bible is completed now we don't need Prophets today.

And what will you Prophecy today the word of God tells you the Past, Present, & Future.

People say they are Prophets today they Prophecy in a crowd say somebody has high blood pressure, sugar diabetic, you have a pain in your body, you need a financial blessing etc. I can do that that's in any crowd you find that's not Prophecy.

The New Testament Prophets &Old Testament Prophets Prophecy things that happened and yet will happen in the future. Read Zechariah: chapter 14. the day of the Lord this is future. the Book of Revelation this is future the anti- Christ New Jerusalem this is future.

Ephesians: Chapter 4. verse 11. continues and some, these 3 Gifts was given for the maturity of the saints.

Pastors:

Teachers:

Evangelists:

so that the saints would grow up & saints will have a ministry the pastor has to equipped them.

evangelists; -means to spread the Gospel you have today.

and some pastors-they Shepherd the people because sheep is ignorant and they need someone to lead them

It doesn't mean you can lead to manage people is different. You have this today.

Teachers- this is not the Natural Gift to teach School people etc. but this is Bible Teaching you don't inherit this God has to give you this Gift we have this Gift today.

In Romans: Chapter 12. verse 6. gift of prophecy Paul said make sure your prophecy from faith -this was faith of the Bible there is no more Prophets today.

Verse 7. Or ministry -means Deacons, yes, we have them today they serve tables and used the office etc.

exhorted- he exhorts people to come. We have today

He that giveth- simply done if he has a Gift of giving. We have Today.

He that ruleth-make sure you're diligent he is the Pastor of the church you have today.

Mercy -show mercy we have today.

cheerfulness-you are cheerful we have today.

<u>So, we don't have Today:</u>

1. Healing
2. Miracles
3. Diver's Kind of tongues
4. Interpretation of Tongues
5. Apostles
6. Prophets

These gifts were foundational Gifts they were temporal gifts in Paul's day in 1st Corinthians chapter 13. verse 9. they only had partial knowledge they had the Old

Testament Paul them was making the New Testament up in his day.

Verse 10. when that which is perfect is come that in part will be done away with. it has we now have the New Testament the whole Bible now all 66 Books the Old and New Testament.

Now the Old Testament was written in Hebrew and The New Testament was written in Greek. this is how we know what Bible today is right or wrong we go back to the original language of that day when the Bible was first written.

God always had a way for you and me to know what's true or false .it just like counterfeit money they look just like the real thing and it's hard to detect but the original show the truth. that what the original language does it detect what true or false and any flaws of the 26 or more Bibles that's out there Today. that's why God left it for us to search it to see the truth and not be deceived like so many is.

So those gifts were temporal we don't need these 6 today because we have the complete Bible it took their place. the Apostles did all these things but they are gone now. They were temporal.

What We do have: today these are permanent:

1. Pastors
2. Evangelists
3. Teachers
4. Ministry-Deacons
5. Discernment of the Spirit- {this is my Gift I can feel when there is something is going to happen to a person when I see you and I don't have to know you that feeling come over me some call its premonition I call it Discernment of the Spirit.}
6. faith
7. Knowledge
8. Wisdom
9. Exhort
10. Giveth
11. Ruleth
12. Mercy
13. Cheerful

You can look back what we have explained what they mean and what we do and do not have today.

Remember Preaching has to be caught not taught - means God has to open your eyes so you can see the truth my prayer is that I be filled with the spirit everyday -means that I be controlled by the spirit every day.

Preparing to Meet the Millennium Reign

Table of Contents:

Part: 1. Accountability of the Saints:
Part: 2. Rewards:
Part: 3. Judgment of The Nations:

Introduction: We that are Christians will not be Judged for sin. in Romans: Chapter 8. verse 1. There is therefore now no condemnation-means no Judgment verse continues to them which are in Christ Jesus, who walk not after the flesh, but after the Spirit.

So now we are in Christ the Judgment has passed for sin and we have peace with God and the war is over for sin because God is at war with sin but now, we have peace with him. and we are working to get our Reward not to be saved. And we are preparing to meet the Millennium Reign we already have salvation.

In John Chapter 3. verse 16. Says for God so loved the world, that he gave his only begotten Son, that whosoever believeth in him should not perish, but have everlasting life. Once you believe you already have eternal life.

Let's look at 3. Things:

1. Justification- means you have made it right with God
2. Sanctification- you put off and put on this is where we are right now. do we sin yes but the blood of Jesus Christ exempts us? the case is dismissed. why because God Judge the intent of the heart not the sins we do. he knew before you accepted him you would sin. so, he cannot see your sins through the Blood.

    In 1st John: Chapter 1. verse 7. says But if we walk in the light, as he is in the light, we have fellowship one with another, and the blood of Jesus Christ his Son cleanseth us from all sin. This is Gods wash basin for the saints after they are saved. when you sin, you don't have to be saved again that's wrong teaching God is too intelligent to have to keep saving you over and over every time you sin.

3. Glorification- we will be Glorified when we die and get out of this body and get our Glorified body this is future.

Part: 1. Accountability of the Saints:

In Matthews: Chapter 25. verse 14. For the kingdom of heaven- means this is the Millennium Kingdom verse continue is as a man travelling into a far country, who called his own servants, and delivered unto them his goods. - This is talking to the saints we are accountable for what God gave you. In verses 14-30 so let's go to work.

Verse 15. And unto one he gave five talents, to another two, and to another one; to every man according to his several ability; and straightway took his journey. So, God gave every Christian something to do according to your ability.

Verse 16. Then he that had received the five talents went and traded with the same and made them other five talents. He went to work that's why this Book is named Preparing to meet the Millennium Reign. Our work we do right now determines if we go into the Millennium Reign.

In Verse 17. And likewise, he that had received two, he also gained other two. He worked to.

Verse 18. But he that had received one went and digged in the earth and hid his lord's money. He didn't use what he got you have to use what God has given to you. Because one day there is going to be a reckoning day and you have to give an account for what you were given.

Verse. 19. After a long time the lord of those servants cometh, and reckoneth with them. This is accountability of the saints.

Verse 20. And so, he that had received five talents came and brought other five talents, saying Lord, thou deliveredst unto me five talents: behold, I have gained beside them five talents more. He went to work.

Verse 21. His Lord said unto him, well done, thou good and faithful servant: thou hast been faithful over a few things, I will make thee ruler over many things: enter thou into the joy of thy lord. He went to work and gained others he has a Thousand Years reward. this is the bema seat some Faithful Servant will be ruler over these things.

Verse. 22. He also that had received two talents came and said, Lord thou deliveredst unto me two talents: behold, I have gained two other talents beside them.

Verse 23. His lord said unto him, well done, good and faithful servant; thou hast been faithful over a few things, I will make thee ruler over many things: enter thou into the joy of thy lord.

This refers to Romans: Chapter 14. Verse 11. For it is written, As I live, saith the Lord, every knee shall bow to me, and every tongue shall confess to God.

Verse 12. So, then every one of us shall give account of himself to God. So, every Christian has to give an account of his works after we are saved.

In 2nd Corinthians: Chapter: 5. Verse 10. Says For we must all appear before the judgment seat- means bema seat this is in heaven for the Christians only verse continue of Christ; that every one may receive the things done in his body, according to that he hath done, whether it be good or bad.

Means we are Judged according to our works after we are saved. And we will know then if we go into the Millennium or not. That why we must prepare now so we can make it into the Millennium Reign.

How do we prepare we have to get busy and stay busy go the work for the Lord? We have gotten satisfied with what we have at the Churches 2 hundred or more members. but we have to leave the walls of the building and go out into the highways and compel people to come. This is why New Churches grow faster than Old Churches. But If we do not, we will miss the Millennium like the slothful Christian.

In Matthews: Chapter: 25. Verse. 24-30 because we got saved and sat down and didn't use what we got.

Verse 24. Then he which had received the one talent came and said, Lord, I knew then that thou art a hard man, reaping where thou hast not sown, and gathering where thou hast not strawed. He made excuses just like Christians are doing today. I don't have time, I work, etc.

Verse 25. And I was afraid and went and hid thy talent in the earth: lo, there thou hast that is thine. He sat down.

Verse 26. His lord answered and said unto him, thou wicked and slothful servant, - means Christian verse continue thou knewest that I reap where I sowed not and gather where I have not strawed:

Verse 27. Thou oughtest therefore to have put my money to the exchangers, and then at my coming I should have received mine own with usury. God expect something in return from us he knows what he invested in you. Verse

28. Take therefore the talent from him and give it unto him which hath ten talents. Give it to someone who will use it and bring others in the Kingdom.

Verse 29. For unto every one that hath shall be given, and he shall have abundance: but from him that hath not shall be taken away even that which he hath. His reward was taken away someone else received that reward.

Verse 30. And cast ye the unprofitable servant- means Christian verse continues into outer darkness-this is not hell like some people say no but the o layer means the outer layer – Verse continues There shall be weeping - means the Christian will be complaining.

And gnashing of the teeth. - means wishing he had not missed the Millennium Reign.

So, he has to sit in outer darkness- the o layer of the earth- means the outer layer of the earth for a Thousand Years. He missed the Millennium Reign. and you can today to if you sit down and be lazy and don't witness for the Lord.

In Matthews 8. Verse 11. And I say unto you, that many shall come from the east and west, and shall sit down with Abraham, and Isaac, and Jacob, in the kingdom of heaven. - means this is At the Millennium Kingdom.

Verse 12. But the children of the kingdom- means Christians verse continues shall be cast into outer darkness: there shall be weeping and gnashing of teeth. This led me to.

Part 2. Rewards:

At the Bema Seat our works will be tried by fire. In 1st Corinthians: Chapter: 3. Verse 12. Now if any man builds upon this foundation gold, silver, precious stones, wood, hay, stubble; –these are 6 different kinds of Christians so which one is you. You know if you are working or not don't deceive yourself get busy while you have time payday is coming.

Verse 13. Every man's work shall declare it, because it shall be revealed by fire; and the fire shall try every man's work of what sort it is. Only Gold, Silver, Precious Stones work will Receive a Reward and Reign with Christ in the Millennium Reign.

Verse 14. If any man's work abide which he hath built thereupon, he shall receive a reward.

Verse 15. If any man's work shall be burned, - wood, hay, stubble they will not be rewarded they will miss the Millennium Reign. they didn't do enough they were slothful and lazy Christians like in Matthews: Chapter: 25. Verses 14-30 they missed the Millennium Reign.

So, let's get busy we don't want to miss out right. I believe that at least half of the Christians will miss the Millennium Reign.

Now 1st Corinthians 3 verse 15 continues but he himself shall be saved - that's the Christian he will be saved but his works is lost.

You see you can lose your reward but not your salvation. And a lot of Christians will. they say all I want is to be saved and that's enough. So, they will do no work for God.

But you should want more a reward is for you to if you earn it. We are not working to be saved we have that already.

You do not have to earn salvation because salvation is free. but you have to earn your Reward you have to work to get it it's. not free. we are working to get our reward.

In Revelation: Chapter: 21. verse. 4. And God shall wipe away all tears from their eyes- these are the ones that missed the Millennium Reign. but you will be in new Jerusalem with God.

Part: 3. Judgment of the Nations:

In Matthews: Chapter :25. Verses 25-31 these are the nations-or people that didn't feed Israel. This will take place when the Lord Return to the Earth he will Judge these nations that mistreated Israel. This is not talking to us right now this is future.

In Matthews: Chapter: 25. Verse 31. When the Son of man shall come in his glory, and all the holy angels with him, then shall he sit upon the throne of his glory: -his throne in the Millennium Kingdom on earth.

Verse 32. And before him shall be gathered all nations: -means people is before the lord. And he shall separate them one from another, as a shepherd divided his sheep from the goats:

Verse 33. And he shall set the sheep on his right hand, - there is no nation made up of sheep. But the goats on the left. - goats yes but this don't mean the United States, Canada, Japan, etc. all these places are before the Lord. It doesn't mean that.

Verse 34. let's Clears this up Then shall the King say unto them on his right hand, come, ye blessed of my Father, inherit the kingdom- it's not these nations but the righteous shall inherit the kingdom these are the sheep. and the goats are the unrighteous. They will go into everlasting fire. there is no sheep and goat nation but this is talking about Righteous and Unrighteous people. prepared for you from the foundation of the world:

Verse 35. For I was an hungred, and ye gave me meat: I was thirsty, and ye gave me drink: I was a stranger, and ye took me in: this is talking to the people that help Israel in that day it's not talking to the people today.

Verse 36. Naked, and ye clothed me: I was sick, and ye visited me: I was in prison, and ye came unto me. These people gave Israel food, clothing, visit them in prison. there is nothing wrong with doing these things today. But this is not telling us today we have to do this. But they did this to Israel and the Lord rewarded them.

Verse 37. Then shall the righteous answer him, saying, Lord when saw we thee an hungred, and fed thee? or thirsty, and gave thee drink?

Verse 38. When saw we thee a stranger, and took thee in? or naked, and clothed thee?

Verse 39. Or when saw we thee sick, or in prison, and came unto thee?

Verse 40. And the King shall answer and say unto them, Verily I say unto you, Inasmuch as ye have done it unto one of the least of these my brethren, -Israel ye have done it unto me. When you helped Israel, you helped me. This was the righteous people on the right side. You see we have already been judged this cannot be us. This determines if they get eternal life.

Verse 41. Then shall he say also unto them on the left hand, depart from me, ye cursed, into everlasting fire, - now this is the lake of fire. Prepared for the devil and his angels. Because you didn't help Israel.

Verse 42. For I was an hungred, and ye gave me no meat: I was thirsty, and ye gave me no drink.

Verse 43. I was a stranger, and ye took me not in: naked, and ye clothed me not: sick and in prison, and ye visited me not. Let me explain this to you. People apply these verses to us today that is wrong application. Jesus never told us we had to go to prisons and have prison ministries or go out and feed the poor and clothed them.

This is good we do this but understand if we do not this will not determine our salvation. This was to the nation -or people in the future Return of the lord they that didn't help Israel.

Verse 44. Then shall they also answer him, saying, Lord, when saw we thee an hungred, or athirst, or a stranger, or naked, or sick, or in prison, and did not minister unto thee?

Verse 45. Then shall he answer them, saying, Verily I say unto you, inasmuch as ye did it not to one of the least of these, -this is Israel not us today okay so do not misinterpret this for you today like so many has ok. ye did it not to me. Helping Israel was like doing it to the Lord.

Verse 46. And these shall go away into everlasting punishment: - the ones on the left will be judged then and into the lake of fire everlasting.

Revelation: chapter: 19. verse 11. And I saw heaven opened and behold a white horse; and he that sat upon him was called Faithful and righteousness he doth judge and make war. - this is the war on the unrighteous. But the righteous- on the right will be judged and go into life eternal.

Revelation: chapter: 19. Verse 15. And out of his mouth goeth a sharp sword, that with it he should smite the nations: and he shall rule-be for the righteous. them with a rod or iron: and he treadeth the winepress of the fierceness and wrath of Almighty God. May God Bless your hearts let's get busy Christians lets Prepare to meet the Millennium Reign.

Rules in The Kingdom of Heaven

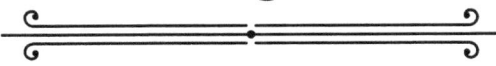

Table of Contents:

Part: 1. Dispensations:
Part:2. Kingdom of God:
Part: 3. Kingdom of Heaven:

Introduction: these are Rules for those in the Kingdom of Heaven this apply in the Future Millennium Reign not today. in The Book of Matthews. there is 2 key thing's we must understand in the Book of Matthews.

1. The difference between the Kingdom of Heaven
2. And the Kingdom of God

Part: 1. Dispensations:

<u>There are 7 Dispensations and all ended in Failure except the Kingdom of Heaven.</u>

1. Innocents: Failed. From Creation of man to his Fall. Genesis Chapter: 1. 3000 BC. Or earlier

Genesis Chapter: 3. verse 7. God dealt with man in his Innocence.
2. Conscience: Failed. with Knowledge eyes come open. Genesis Chapter 4. verse 7. From Eden to the Flood.
3. Human Government: Failed. man, governed man he governed the earth. Genesis: Chapter: 8. verse 15. from the Flood to Babel.
4. Promise: Failed. From Noah to the Call of Abraham to Egyptian Bondage. Genesis: Chapter: 12. verse 1.
5. Law: Failed. Had no love in it. From Mount Sinai to Calvary. Exodus: Chapter: 19. verse 1.
6. Grace: Failed. From Pentecost to the Second Coming of Christ. Matthew: Chapter 1.
7. Kingdom of Heaven: From the Kingdom / Judgment of the Nations to New Jerusalem. Matthews: Chapter: 25. verse 31-46 to Revelation: Chapter: 21.

So, we see there is 7 Dispensations and today we are under Grace it will end when the Church is Rapture up -Rapture means- caught up. In 1ˢᵗ Thessalonians: Chapter: 4. verse 16. Says for the Lord himself shall descend from heaven with a shout, with the voice of the archangel, and with the trump of God: and the dead in Christ shall rise first: this is the Resurrection of the dead Christians bodies.

Verse 17. Then we which are alive and remain shall be caught up together with them in the clouds, to meet the Lord in the air: and so, shall we ever be with the Lord.

This is the Rapture of the saints and we which are alive shall be caught up- means Rapture up together with them – means the other dead saints.

you see some of us will be alive when the Rapture takes place it will be a generation alive that will not die a physical death when Jesus comes in the air. it can happen any day now. We will meet Christ in the air. his feet will not touch the earth this time.

But it will in the future in Zechariah: chapter: 14. verse 4. His feet shall stand in that day upon the mount of Olives, which is before Jerusalem on the east, and the mount of Olives shall cleave in the midst thereof toward the east and toward the west, and there shall be a very great valley; and half of the mountain shall remove toward the north, and half of it toward the south.

This is the Return of the Lord to the earth and we know where he is coming to Jerusalem. This takes place after the Battle of Armageddon in Zechariah Chapter: 14. verse 2&3. At the End of this Dispensation of Grace this age.

In Matthews: Chapter: 13. verse 43. Then shall the righteous shine forth as the sun in the Kingdom of their Father. Who hath ears to hear, let him hear. -this is during the Millennium Reign the 1,000 years on earth.

We must remember that Jesus left here on the mount of olives in Acts Chapter: 1. verse 9. And when he- means Jesus had spoken these things, while they beheld, he was taken up; and a cloud received him out of their sight.

Verse 10. And while they looked steadfastly toward heaven as he went up, behold, two men stood by them in white apparel;

Verse 11. Which also said, Ye men of Galilee, why stand ye gazing up into heaven? This same Jesus, which is taken up from you into heaven, -means Jesus left here from the mount of olives. Verse continues shall so come-means back to the mount of olives like he left this will be fulfilled in the future in Zechariah Chapter: 14. verse 4. Verse continues in like manner as ye have seen him go into heaven.

Verse 12. Then returned they unto Jerusalem from the mount called Olivet, -means they were at the mount of olives. Verse continues Which is from Jerusalem a Sabbath day's journey.

Part: 2. Kingdom of God:

The Kingdom of God we have now when we accepted Jesus Christ in our lives that put us in the Kingdom of a God. And anywhere you see the word Kingdom of God in the Book of Matthews: Chapter: 6. verse 33. Says But seek ye first the kingdom of God, and his righteousness; and all these things shall be added unto you- means seek to do Gods will- means seek to get people saved and he will take care of our business. The Kingdom of God it means now under Grace we are in it.

Part: 3. Kingdom of Heaven:

In these chapters these are Rules for the Kingdom of Heaven -this is the Millennium Kingdom -Thousand Years period on earth. These Rules is during the Thousand Years of Peace on Earth. And we will have a Glorified Body and then we will be able to do or take these sufferings we won't be in this fleshly body. We will have a Glorified Body But not for us now this is future. This leads me to Rules in the Kingdom of Heaven.

In Matthews: Chapter: 5. We call these the Beatitudes- they are for the future not now we misinterpret this and use these in verses 2-11 for us today not so. The key is in verse 3. Kingdom of Heaven. so, when you see Kingdom of Heaven- that means during the 1,000 Years on Earth. that is Future that do not apply to us today.

Verse 1. And seeing the multitudes, he-is Jesus went up into a mountain: and when he was set, his disciples came unto him:

Verse 2. And he opened his mouth, and taught them, saying, -now he gives rules to the Disciples concerning the Millennial Kingdom.

Verse 3. Blessed are the poor in spirit: for their's is the kingdom of heaven -this is Future in the Millennium.

Verse 4. Blessed are they that mourn: - for they shall be comforted. - remember during the 1,000 years there will be peace on earth.

5. Blessed are the meek: for they shall inherit the earth. - during the 1,000 years.

6. Blessed are they which do hunger and thirst after righteousness: for they shall be filled. -this is future

7. Blessed are the merciful: for they shall obtain mercy. – this is future.

8. Blessed are the pure in heart: for they shall see God. – this is future

9. Blessed are the peacemakers: for they shall be called the children of God. – this is future.

10. Blessed are they which are persecuted for righteousness' sake: for their's is the kingdom of heaven. -there is that word again that how we know these 9 Blessed are talking about during the Millennium Reign.

11. Blessed are ye, when men shall revile you, and persecute you, and shall say all manner of evil against you falsely, for my sake.

This is why I talk about in my 1st Book I wrote the Apostolic Age: when you study the Bible find out

<u>3 things.</u>

1. Who it's talking to
2. What it's saying
3. When it was said.

Now let go down to Chapter 5. Jesus is giving Rules again. In Matthew: Chapter: 5. Verse. 38 Ye have heard that it hath been said, an eye for an eye, and a tooth for tooth: -he is talking about the law here but

In Verse 39. But I say unto you, that ye resist not evil: but whosoever shall smite thee on thy right cheek, turn to him the other also. - he never told us to do this today in our times. He never told you to turn the other cheek. You are not able to do that right now. But in the future during the Millennium, you will be able to. This is future.

Verse 40. And if any man will sue thee at the law, and take away thy coat, let him have thy cloke also this is future.

Verse 41. And whosoever shall compel thee to go a mile, go with him twain- means 2 miles. This is future. These are Jesus Rules in the Millennium Kingdom- Thousand years period in the future.

Let's look at Matthews: Chapter: 6. verse 1. Take heed that ye do not your alms before men, to be seen of them: otherwise ye have no reward of your Father which is in heaven.

Verse 9. This is the Disciples Prayer Jesus he gave it to them to pray. This is not to us to pray but to the Disciples. Verse 9 continues After this manner therefore pray ye: Our Father- is God which art in heaven, Hallowed- means holly be thy name.

Verse 10. Thy kingdom come. -this is the Millennium Kingdom which is future when we Reign on Earth for a Thousand Years. verse continues Thy will be done in earth, as it is in heaven.

Verse 11. Give us this day our daily bread.

Verse 12. And forgive us our debts, as we forgive our debtors.

Verse 13. And lead us not into temptation but deliver us from evil: For thine is the kingdom, - means Millennium Kingdom they will be in the kingdom one day and so will some of us not all Christians will be in the Millennium because of their works.

I will tell you more about it in my next Book. Preparing to Meet the Millennium Reign: you need to buy it.

Verse 13. continues and the power, and the glory, forever. Amen. so, you see this Prayer was to the Disciples not us.

In John: Chapter 17. Verse 1-26 this is the Lord's Prayer Jesus prayed this prayer because his hour had come. I say to you today if you have time to pray when your hour-time to die. Come ask Jesus to forgive you for all of your sins and receive my spirit unto thee this prayer we should pray today May God Bless your hearts.

The Curse of Nature

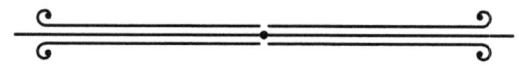

Table of Contents:

Part: 1. The Creator:
Part: 2. The Creature:
Part: 3. The Curse:

Introduction: Man started keeping record around 3,000 B.C. now Evolution has to be repeated but History- human history you cannot repeat it. Scientist cannot take nothing and make something they have to start with something. But God can. the problem with Evolution is Time is the key thing. The problem with Evolution is the Formula- Mutation & Natural Selection x Time = Evolution.

1. Problems are Mutation: - is a small change in your DNA your Genes causing them to different from their parent's and well-marked characteristics. when you look at us, we don't have well marked characteristics. different characteristics that are passed on. some of us favor our mom and some favor our grandparents.

2. Natural Selection: - The mechanism that preserves the changes caused by mutations.
3. Time: - Long - period of time are necessary for this to take place.

Evolution: - is a Religion time is the key thing with Evolutionist.

there is a word called Apologetics: - is the Defense of the truth of Christianity. When you stand to defend a whole lot of folk's will leave you. 99% is the truths of Christianity 1% I make up.

the Earth is only a few thousand years old not millions according to the Bible. and Scientist is finding that out.

Part: 1. The Creator:

Is God he is Sovereign-mean's he pick's and choose what he wants to do. So, in Genesis: Chapter: 1. verse. 26. And God said, let us- is the trinity 3 in one the Father, the Son, and the Holy Ghost, they were all there. Verse continues make man- the creature is man. We will talk about the creature next. Verse continues in our image, after our likeness: and let them have dominion over the fish of the sea, and over the fowl of the air, and over the cattle, and over all the earth, and over every creeping thing that creepeth upon the earth. So, God made man a conquer of all things.

Verse 27. So, God created man in his own image, in the image of God created he him: male and female created he them. So, man didn't come from an ape God created them man and woman. In Genesis: Chapter: 2. Verse 7. And the Lord God formed man of the dust of the ground and breathed into his nostril the breath of life; and man became a living soul.

Go back to verse 21.

Verse 21. And the Lord God caused a deep sleep to fall upon Adam, and he slept: and he took one of his ribs and closed up the flesh instead thereof: verse

22. And the rib, which the Lord God had taken from man, made he a woman, and brought her unto the man. So, we see the woman was made from the man.

Verse 23. And Adam said, this is now bone of my bones, and flesh of my flesh: she shall be called Woman, because she was taken out of Man.

So, Adam named her Woman and he named every living creature.

So, man and woman did Not come from an ape don't believe that believe the Bible its right Scientist is wrong.

So, God- is the Creator and is the 1st cause in Genesis: Chapter: 1. verse 1. In the beginning God created the heaven and the earth.

Verse 2. And the earth was without form, and void; and darkness was upon the face of the deep. And the Spirit of God moved upon the face of the waters.

Let's look at causes and effects- we never see the cause but we see the effects of things.

In Genesis: Chapter: 1. verse 2. So, we see the effects of the earth but what cause it to be without form or void.

Example cause- car wreck break fails other cars of the cause.

A car comes from metal, and metal, comes from the earth, and the earth, comes from God.

God is 1st cause everything comes from him.

In Ecclesiastes: Chapter: 12. Verse 1. Remember now thy Creator- means God verse continues in the days of thy youth, while the evil days come not, nor the years draw nigh, when thou shalt say, I have no pleasure in them. This leads me to.

Part: 2. The Creature:

Genesis: Chapter: 1. verse 25. And God made the beast of the earth after his kind, and cattle after their kind, and everything that creepeth upon the earth after his kind: and God saw that it was good.

This included the Dinosaur as well if they existed, I believe they all died during the flood in Noah day. Every creature that was created man tamed until man sinned in the Garden. Today man still tame animals and they turn on him because of the Curse.

Man is also called a creature because he was created like the animals and other creatures. we are not greater than the creator. We will talk next about the creation.

Man is finite: - means he is limited but

God is infinite: - God is unlimited

man is also rational: - means he can reason he can think

but the animals they are irrational: - means they react off their instincts that's why man can conquer them.

But God conquers all. In Isaiah: Chapter 55. Verse 8. For my thoughts are not your thoughts, neither are your ways my ways, saith the Lord.

Verse 9. For as the heavens are higher than the earth, so are my ways higher than your ways, and my thoughts than your thoughts. It's like we are inside a circle and God is outside all by himself. This leads me to.

Part: 3. The Curse of Nature:

This is where most of my time will be spent in this book. This is the title of the book. in Romans: Chapter: 1. Verse 20. For the invisible things of him from the creation of the world are clearly seen, being understood by the things that are made - creation itself tells us there is a God we can see from the elements the sun, moon, stars, etc.

We must remember that where there is a Design there has to be a mind. And intelligence is housed in a mind. no man can design those elements- there has to be a higher power and that's God Almighty. Even his eternal power and Godhead; so that they are without excuse: so, there is no excuse that there is a God.

Creation tells you and God reveals himself to you in some way a dream, etc. even to people that don't have a Bible to read in other countries. so, there is no excuse.

Since the Fall of Man, the earth has been cursed - it out of whack with thorns and thistles and all kinds of insect's pest and diseases germs, and man by the sweat of his face has been compelled to earn his daily bread. This is why we get sick and we die because of the curse.

In Romans: Chapter: 8. Verse 22. For we know that the whole creation groaneth and travailed in pain together until now. This is the curse of nature. One day it will be lifted.

<u>The Curse was fourfold:</u>

1. The Serpent: - the snake in Genesis: Chapter: 3. Verse 14. And the Lord God said unto the serpent, because thou hast done this, thou art cursed above all cattle, and above every beast of the field; upon thy belly shalt thou go, and dust shalt thou eat all the days of thy life. The snake was satins tool he used. it was beautiful and attractive it uses to stand up on its feet. But now it has to crawl upon its belly and eat dust.
2. The Woman: - in verse 16. Unto the woman he said, I will greatly multiply thy sorrow and thy conception; - children born in sorrow thou shalt

bring forth children; and thy desire – means woman today desire to rule the man. Verse continues shall be to thy husband, and he shall rule over thee.

Woman was created equal of man, but because she caused him to fall, she lost her equality and man was given the Headship over her. In 1st Peter: Chapter: 3. Verse 7. Likewise, ye husbands, dwell with them according to knowledge, giving honour unto the wife, as unto the weaker vessel, – means she cannot discern like the man.

you see that from Genesis. Verse 7. continues and as being heirs together of the grace of life; that your prayers be not hindered.

3. The Man: - verse 17. And unto Adam he said, because thou hast hearkened unto the voice of thy wife, and hast eaten of the tree, of which I commanded thee, saying, thou shalt not eat of it: cursed is the ground for thy sake; in sorrow shalt thou eat of it all the days of thy life; the ground was cursed and now man has to work hard labor and sweat.

4. The Ground: - verse 18. Thorns also and thistles shall it bring forth to thee; and thou shalt eat the herb of the field -these herbs became tainted

after man sinned today man has discovered many ways to use these herbs example marijuana etc. this idea came from satin. From the beginning God never intended for man to use his herbs that way sin caused that.

Verse 19. In the sweat of thy face shalt thou eat bread, till thou return unto the ground; for out of it wast thou taken: -means created from dust thou art and unto dust shalt thou return. This made it difficult for man he had to work hard now. Which would wear out his system and end in physical death. Now the Curse of Nature will be lifted during the Millennial Reign - this is the Thousand Years period

In Isaiah: Chapter: 35. Verse 1. The wilderness and the solitary place shall be glad for them; and the desert shall rejoice, and blossom as the rose.

In Psalms: Chapter: 67. Verse 6. Then shall the earth yield her increase; and God, even our own God, shall bless us.

In Amos: Chapter: 9. Verse 13. Behold, the days come, saith the Lord that the plowman shall overtake the reaper, and the treader of grapes him that soweth seed; and the mountain shall drop sweet wine, and all the hills shall melt. So, we see in these verses that nature will be restored like it was in Adam and Eve day before the curse.

In Isaiah Chapter: 55. Verse 13. Instead of the thorn shall come up the fir tree, and instead of the brier shall come up the myrtle tree: and it shall be to the Lord for a name, for an everlasting sign that shall not be cut off. So, the earth here will be restored back.

In Isaiah: Chapter: 11. Verse 6. There will be changes in the animal kingdom. The wolf also shall dwell with the lamb, and the leopard shall lie down with the kid; and the calf and the young lion and the fatling together; and a little child shall lead them.

Verse 7. And the cow and the bear shall feed; their young ones shall lie down together: and the lion shall eat straw like the ox. Verse 8. And the sucking child- baby shall play on the hole of the asp, - the snake and the weaned child- child off the bottle shall put his hand on the cockatrice den.

Verse 9. They shall not hurt nor destroy in all my holy mountain: - Jerusalem for the earth shall be full of the knowledge of the Lord, as the waters cover the sea. This is future it will be peace on earth for a Thousand Years even the animals will be at peace among themselves also. It will be like it was before the fall of man. Human life will be restored and you shall live as long as they did before the Flood.

In Isaiah: Chapter: 65. Verse 20. There shall be no more thence- then an infant- baby of days, nor an old man that hath not filled his days: for the child shall die a hundred years old; but the sinner being a hundred years old shall be accursed.

So, we see that a person dying 100 years old shall be considered only a child. Therefore, a man, to be called a man, must live for several hundred years. Yes, people will be being born and are not saved they are sinners and they will die accursed. Satin will be bound and people will still be being born that never Knew about satin.

in Revelation: Chapter: 20 verses. 7. And when the thousand years are expired, Satan shall be loosed out of his prison,

Verse 8. And shall go out to deceive the nations which are in the four quarters of the earth, Gog and Magog, to gather them together to battle: the number of whom is as the sand of the sea.

In Isaiah: Chapter: 65. Verse 22. They shall not build, and another inhabit; they shall not plant, and another eat: for as the days of a tree are the days of my people, and mine elect shall long enjoy the work of their hands. Man will live to be as old as trees. Just like Noah did in Genesis: Chapter: 9. Verse 29. And all the days of Noah were nine hundred and fifty years: and he died.

So that's coming back again. the curse of nature and the animal kingdom will be lifted but not from death and sin yet.

I thank God for the Illumination of his word I pray you have an open heart and mind when you read this book. And that I continue to be filled with his spirit- means- controlled by his spirit may God Bless Your Heart's.

www.ingramcontent.com/pod-product-compliance
Ingram Content Group UK Ltd.
Pitfield, Milton Keynes, MK11 3LW, UK
UKHW050411240426
12048UKWH00020B/1460